I0539134

What's in the Fridge?

Dorm

By Jill Effron

Copyright © 2025 by Jill Effron

Published & Distributed by **Jill Effron**

First Edition: ISBN: 979-8-218-64989-0

PO Box 9277

Marina Del Rey, California 90295

whatsinthedormfridge@gmail.com

Photography & Food Styling: **Jill Effron**

Book Design & Composition: **Robyn Huth**

Editors: **Sara Cohen Fidler** & **Hilary Feldstein Ratner**

 @whatsinthedormfridge

All rights reserved.

This book or any portion thereof may not be reproduced or used in any manner whatsoever without the express written permission of the publisher.

What's in the dorm fridge?

To Avery:

You inspired me to become a personal chef and cooking instructor so I could spend more time at home with you. Now, as you head off to college you have inspired me to write this book for you, your friends, and all the other kids leaving the nest.

I love you and will miss the mess you make in my kitchen.

Have the best time at school!

Love,
Mom, Jill, Juju, Girly-pop ♡

CONTENTS

Introduction

Breakfast

Snacks

Lunch & Dinner

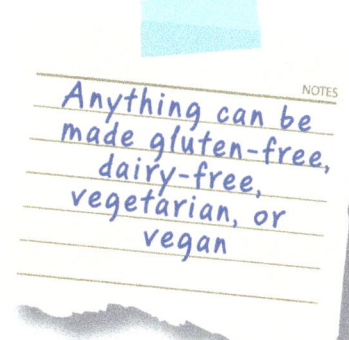

Pita Pocket with Turkey: page 52

Drinks

Get Organized!

> NOTES
> Anything can be made gluten-free, dairy-free, vegetarian, or vegan

Testimonials
From Actual College Kids...

Tonight my roommate and I made your Mediterranean pita pizza recipe! We used a mason jar to shake the ingredients together, which helped to minimize the cleanup! The mix itself was delicious and it was a nice change from the greasy heavy food on campus. Everyone was asking us about what we were making and I told them about your recipes... Thank you so much!! It was so much fun to make and I already made it again with just feta and hummus after running out of veggies! I love the addition of Mediterranean pita pizza!

~Teddy B., Cal Poly SLO

The recipes were both quick and easy -- perfect for a college student on the go. As a senior, I am very busy with school, Greek life commitments, research commitments, and other activities. I'm always looking for new recipes to try out. These recipes were not only quick and easy, but also delicious.

~Alyssa A., Tulane University

I loved the teriyaki chicken because it was a delicious way to incorporate veggies and protein into a yummy carby base. It's always hard to find full recipes that work in the microwave, and these are easy and delicious. Plus, having experience throwing together recipes with a microwave is good practice for when you move into an apartment with a real kitchen!

~Jocelyn M., Northwestern University

Kitchen Counter Storytime

It was a lazy winter break when my daughter emerged from her lair with her hoodie pulled tight across her head and slid onto a stool at our kitchen counter and lamented, "How am I going to leave my dorm room to get food when I'm cold and tired?" A smile crept onto my face. I ran to my desk, grabbed the rough draft of this cookbook, and stood in front of her. She looked down at me - not because she doesn't believe in me, but because she is now significantly taller than me. I held the book up and said, "I got you." She smiled.

When I was in college in the early '90s, my dorm room fridge was filled with half and half for my coffee that I would mix with a packet of hot chocolate, plus a tub of butter and milk for my box of mac and cheese that I would cook on the dorm kitchen stove. And in the freezer was a stash of frozen French bread pizza. That was it!!

Since my daughter is off to college, I wanted to come up with (mostly) healthy recipes that can be prepared easily in a dorm room or dorm kitchen. In fact, if you can make these recipes in a dorm room, you can make them anywhere. My hope is that this book will be with you as you move into different kitchens in your life. The more you practice and experiment in the kitchen, the more you will become confident. Kitchen confidence lasts forever and is a skill you will use every single day of your life. In time you will be able to look at a full or bare fridge or pantry and throw together a meal like a chef!

With my background as a personal chef and cooking instructor for my business What's in the Fridge?, I have had people of all ages test out these recipes. Sometimes this was at my kitchen table, my son's pre-k class, and then on Zoom throughout the quarantine era. And now some of the teens I taught online are off to college and were also the inspiration to create this book, What's in the Dorm Fridge?

So, to all of the tired and cold future and current dorm-dwellers, I got you!

Let's get cooking!

~ Jill

Cooking 101

Throughout this book you will see little notes from me with reminders, maybe "momsplaining" some things or dropping some hints. That's just me virtually looking over your shoulder trying to anticipate any questions you may have, but also giving you space to find your own inner chef. Also, please feel free to adjust any recipe to your lifestyle and taste! That's the true beauty in cooking for yourself.

NOTES

I say "Ramekin" throughout this book which is a 6-8 oz small bowl with many purposes: scrambling an egg, cooking an egg in the microwave or toaster oven, and holding portion-sized snacks.

"Ramekin"

If you are using an air fryer, follow the toaster oven instructions, it will cook faster

Dorm Tips & Tricks!

Little things to help you stock your dorm room while keeping your costs down.

-When you order take-out... and you will, save the soy sauce packets, the parm cheese containers, red chili flakes, extra sides of dressing, napkins, etc. You will use them down the road.

-When ordering Asian food, order an extra container of white rice. It will save you time and a pot to clean. In particular, it will be perfect for the teriyaki bowl recipe or just add some frozen peas, soy sauce, and a scrambled egg to it and voila!... a quick not-fried, fried rice!

NOTES

THE MICROWAVE:
Please remember not to use metal in it.

THE TOASTER OVEN:
Please remember not to use a metal object to retrieve your food. There's not enough gel on the market to tame electrocuted hair.

THE STOVETOP:
Please keep your hair back! No dangling sleeves. Once you are done with the pot or pan, remove it from the burner to prevent burning the bottom. Do not place it on a countertop as it will scorch or crack the countertop. Your parents do not want to pay to replace a countertop.

One
More
Thing

Before
You
Start

NOTES

FYI
tsp = teaspoon
tbsp = tablespoon
c = cup

Rules

Wax paper cannot go into an oven; it is to wrap food for the fridge. Parchment paper can do **both**.

Clean hands are the best tools. After handling raw food, wash yer hands!

Label your food with dates so you know when you opened a jar or made a dish. This prevents waste.

Microwave your sponges for one minute and wash your dishtowels to kill germs.

Wash your utensils and cookware with soap and hot water.

Do not microwave plastic. Put it into a microwave-safe glass container.

Your fridge temperature should be set at 40 degrees or lower.

Cool leftovers before refrigerating. Excess bacteria can grow. Hot food can raise the temperature of your fridge, which may accelerate the spoiling of your refrigerated items.

Cooked food or perishables should not sit out for more than two hours.

Remember to unplug your appliances after using them, hot plates, etc. once you are finished using them.

Balanced Snack Ideas

If the thought of cooking feels too much at this time, here is a chart to help you create some solid, balanced snacks that you can easily make in your dorm room. You can mix and match from different columns to create new snack ideas.

Carbs (Choose 1)	Protein/Fats (Choose 1 or 2)	Veggies & Fruit (Choose 1 or 2)
Rice Cakes	Nut Butter	Banana Slices
Whole Wheat Bread	Cream Cheese	Cucumber Slices
Pasta w/ Olive Oil	Parmesan Cheese	Cherry Tomatoes
Woven Wheat Crackers	Cheddar Cheese, Nuts	Apples & Grapes
Brown or White Rice	Seaweed & Avocado	Snap Peas & Cucumber
Tortilla Chips	Monterey Jack Cheese	Tomatoes & Avocado
Whole Wheat Pita	Chicken, Turkey, Ham, Your Favorite Cheese	Lettuce & Carrots
Low-Sugar Granola	Plain Greek Yogurt, Nuts	Fresh or Frozen Berries
Tortillas	Black beans, Cheddar Cheese	Tomatoes & Avocado
Naan	Hard Boiled Eggs & Feta	Watermelon
Whole Grain Cereal	Milk	Bananas & Blueberries
Pita Chips	Hummus	Carrot & Celery Sticks
Crackers	Cottage Cheese	Melon

Breakfast Tacos on Blue Corn Tortillas: page 16

How To Make Eggs:
The Most Versatile Food

Eggs are an excellent source of protein. I have provided many different egg recipes you can make in your dorm room using the microwave, a toaster oven, or the stovetop. You do not have to keep a dozen eggs in your fridge. You can buy a carton of 6, or you can buy liquid eggs that come in a resealable container. There are also vegan options on the market. If you do not want to cook with eggs and do want to eat eggs, many grocery stores carry pre-boiled eggs in the refrigerated section.

Eggs have Rules!

1. Always wash your hands after touching raw eggs – you don't have time for salmonella. You have a test next week in that class you don't "love."

2. Always switch utensils when working with raw and cooked eggs. If you scramble an egg with one fork, use a different fork to remove your cooked eggs from the ramekin or pan and for eating said cooked egg. Again, no time for foodborne illnesses – you have finals!! Did you study yet?!

3. The same rules apply when you work with any raw meat products. Use one utensil and plate for raw meat and a different utensil and plate for the cooked meat. Do not cross contaminate!

Scrambled Eggs

Prep & cook time: 5 minutes, serves 1

INGREDIENTS for SCRAMBLED EGGS:
1-2 **eggs**
Salt and **pepper** to taste
1 tsp of **butter**

DIRECTIONS:

Grease your ramekin or mug with a bit of butter. This will help the egg not to stick.

Crack the egg(s) into a ramekin or mug. Check for shells!
Or pour from a carton, follow their instructions on measurements.

Scramble with a fork until the whites and yellows are combined.
Add a pinch of salt and pepper.

Microwave for 20-30 seconds, remove and stir with the raw egg fork, and return to the microwave for 30 seconds. Continue until the eggs are fully cooked and scrambled. Once they are cooked, use a new fork to break them up into scrambled egg pieces. This will take 1 to 1½ minutes - depending on how many eggs you use.

Remove the ramekin using a potholder as the dish can get very hot.

Now you know how to make scrambled eggs!

cont...

Scrambled Eggs

DIRECTIONS:

Grease your ramekin with a bit of butter.

See steps 2 and 3 from the microwave instructions on prior page.

Bake the eggs in the ramekin at 350 degrees for roughly 10-12 minutes, stirring every 4 minutes until cooked.

Turn off the toaster oven and use a potholder to remove the ramekin, then stir the eggs, and place back into the toaster to continue cooking if need be.

DIRECTIONS:

Place a small frying pan over medium heat.

Add 1 teaspoon of butter to coat the entire pan or use cooking spray.

Add in the eggs and then gently stir with a rubber spatula until they begin to firm up on the sides. Bring the cooked sides into the middle of the pan and let the loose eggs go to the sides. Keep doing this until the eggs are cooked to a preferred consistency.

Fried Eggs

DIRECTIONS:

Heat the butter in the pan and once it is melted, crack an egg or two into the pan and season with salt and pepper. When the edges start to crisp up, or the whites start to solidify, use a spatula to flip the egg if you like a solid yolk. Otherwise, cover with a lid until the white is cooked and the yolk is still runny.

Hard Boiled Eggs

DIRECTIONS:

Add 1-2 eggs to a small pot. Cover with water and bring to a boil for 6-10 minutes. 6 minutes for a runny egg, 8 minutes for a jammy egg, 10 minutes for a solid yolk. Once your timer goes off, drain the hot water and add cool water to the pot and let the eggs sit for a few minutes. This will make the egg peeling process easier and stop the eggs from overcooking. Make a bunch to keep in your fridge as a quick snack, or to add to a salad, or to ramen.

Breakfast Sandwich

Prep & cook time: 10-15 minutes, serves 1

INGREDIENTS:
Choose: **bagel**, **English muffin**, 2 slices of **bread** or a **pita**
1 **scrambled** or **fried egg**
1-2 slices of **cheese**

Add-Ins and Optional Toppings:
* sausage patty * sliced tomato or avocado * bacon from a to-go order? *

DIRECTIONS:
See page 13 for scrambled eggs or page 14 fried eggs.
Add cheese to one half of the bread and place into the microwave for 5-10 seconds until the cheese is melted and the bread is warm.
If making sausage, cook according to the package.
Add the egg to one half of the cheesy bread along with any other toppings you may be using.
Close the sandwich, cut it in half, or eat it as is.

NOTE: The eggs, sausage and bread of choice, (with or without cheese), can be cooked all at once in the toaster oven. Just take them out as they are done.

DIRECTIONS:
See page 14 for scrambled or fried eggs.
Add cheese to one of both sides of the bread and toast for 2 minutes or until melted.
See steps 3-5 under microwave.

Breakfast Tacos & Quesadillas

Basically, the same ingredients you would use in a breakfast taco you would use in a breakfast quesadilla. And basically, a breakfast taco is an open-faced breakfast quesadilla when it comes down to it, you know?

Prep & cook time: 10-15 minutes, serves 1

INGREDIENTS:

1-2 flour, corn, or gluten-free **tortillas**
1-2 scrambled **eggs**
2 tbsp or more of shredded Monterey Jack, cheddar, or dairy-free **cheese**
1 tsp of **butter** or cooking spray

Add-Ins and Optional Toppings:

* spinach * caramelized onions * diced breakfast sausage links or patties *
* chopped tomato * guacamole * diced avocado * avocado slices * salsa *
* sour cream * cilantro * green onion * sliced jalapenos *

DIRECTIONS:

See pages 13-14 for directions on how to cook an eggs.
Note: The eggs, sausage, and tortillas can be cooked all at once in the toaster oven. Just take them out as they are done.
Place the tortillas on a paper towel or microwave-safe plate and top with a sprinkle of cheese on each. Microwave for 5-10 seconds or toast for 1-2 minutes to melt the cheese. Careful not to microwave for too long because the tortilla can dry out!
Or place a tortilla on aluminum foil or parchment paper, sprinkle cheese on top, and toast for a minute or until just melted.
Remove the tortillas from the microwave or toaster oven and spoon the eggs and other add-ins on one side of the tortilla and add more cheese on top. Microwave for 10 seconds or toast for 2 minutes to melt the cheese.
Remove from the microwave or toaster oven and close the tortilla and lightly press down to form a half moon quesadilla. Cut in half or in quarters. See? Geometry has finally paid off!
Repeat with the rest of the tortillas.
Serve with any of the topping options listed above.

DIRECTIONS:

See pages 13-14 for directions on how to cook eggs.

Place the cooked eggs on a plate, wiped out the pan, and add a teaspoon of butter or cooking spray to the pan and place over medium heat.

Once the butter has melted, add the tortilla and a sprinkling of cheese on top.

Spoon the eggs and any of the add-ins on one side of the tortilla. Then more cheese.

Fold the eggless side over onto the eggs. Lightly press down to seal - the cheese will act as the glue. After a minute, flip it over and press down to get each side toasty.

Remove the quesadilla and place on the plate to cut in half or quarters. Repeat with remaining tortillas.

Serve with any of the topping options listed above.

How to ^{Efficiently} use a Loaf of Bread

I think most people look at a loaf of bread and either think, "toast and jam," or "PB & J." But here are some ideas to help you utilize an entire loaf of bread so there is not any waste. If you have a loaf of bread, you will always have something hearty to make for any time of day. Grilled cheese is not listed because it deserves its own page. I would never disrespect the best sandwich ever.

These toasts serve 1

Cinnamon Toast

INGREDIENTS:
1 tbsp of **sugar**
1 tsp of **cinnamon**
2 tsp of **butter**
1-2 pieces of **bread**

NOTES

Don't want to measure? Add more sugar than cinnamon to a bowl, stir, then sprinkle on the bread.

DIRECTIONS:
Combine the cinnamon and sugar in a small ramekin.
Toast the bread or not, then spread the butter on each slice.
Sprinkle a thin layer of the cinnamon-sugar mixture on top of the bread or toast.
Cut into triangles or eat as is.

Avocado Toast

INGREDIENTS:
1 **avocado**
Sprinkle of table or **sea salt**

Optional Toppings:
* halved cherry tomatoes * sliced tomato *
* everything bagel seasoning *
* olive oil * feta * eggs *

Important Tips & Tricks:
When cutting an avocado, use a cutting board or a plate. All you do is slice it length-wise around, then twist, and you have halved your avocado. Squeeze the half with the pit so it pops out. Bam!

NOTES

Do not cut an avocado in your hand or you could wind up with "avocado hand" — look it up!

DIRECTIONS:
Toast the bread or leave it as is.
Slice and fan out the avocado onto the bread. Or scoop it out and mash it on the bread until you get a smooth consistency.
Sprinkle with salt or add any topping from the optional toppings list.
Cut the toast in half, on a diagonal, in triangles, in rectangles or in squares! Or not at all!

Loaded Toast

INGREDIENTS:
1-2 slices of **bread**
Any kind of **nut** or **sun butter**
Banana slices, strawberry slices... **bacon?**
Honey
Hemp, chia, or **flax seeds**

Nut Butter is Protein-Packed!

DIRECTIONS:
Place the bread on a plate and spread nut or sun butter on top.
Add sliced banana or strawberries or both.
Drizzle with honey and sprinkle with flax, chia, or hemp seeds.
Cut it or don't. But enjoy!

PB & J

Spread peanut butter (or any nut or sun butter) on one slice and then jelly on the other slice. Close them together and cut. Slice off the crusts and press the edges together to create a crust-less sandwich.

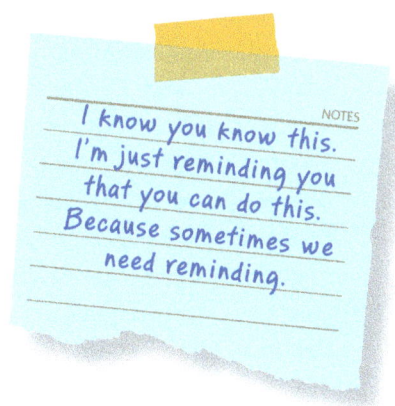

Ricotta Toast

Toast the bread, spread some ricotta on top, and add a drizzle of honey or hot honey. Or add chopped tomatoes, a drizzle of olive oil, and a sprinkle of salt. Or heat up the ricotta in a ramekin in the toaster oven or microwave, and dip crackers or bread into it.

Standard Sandwiches

Get creative... deli meat, cheese, spreads, veggies tucked in between two pieces of bread.

NOTES

I know you know this. I'm just reminding you that you can do this. Because sometimes we need reminding.

Fancy Some Tea Sandwiches?

Spread some leftover cream cheese from that bagel place on your bread. Arrange thinly sliced cucumbers on top. Cut the bread into thirds. Pinky up, take a bite, and sip some tea.

French Toast Two Ways

Prep & cook time: 15-30 minutes, serves 1

INGREDIENTS:
1 **egg**
Splash of **milk**
Splash of **syrup**
Drop of **vanilla** - optional
Sprinkle of **cinnamon**
Pinch of kosher or sea **salt**
2-3 tsp of **butter** or more if needed
1-2 slices of **challah** or any **bread**

Optional Toppings:
* berries * sliced bananas * sliced peaches * powdered sugar *
* maple syrup * chopped nuts *

NOTES

You will only need one slice of bread for the toaster oven French toast and just a little butter to grease the ramekin.

DIRECTIONS:

Grease the ramekin with butter.
Crack an egg into the ramekin then add a splash of milk, a drop of syrup, a dash of vanilla - if you have it - a sprinkle of cinnamon, and a pinch of salt.
Use a fork to beat the ingredients together until everything is incorporated.
Cut a slice of bread into squares.
Place the bread squares into the egg mixture and use your fork to press down on the bread to soak it. If there's too much egg, add a few more bread cubes.
Let the bread soak in the mix for 2 minutes.
Place the ramekin in the toaster oven at 350 degrees and bake for 20-25 minutes or until the top is puffy and golden brown and there is no more raw egg.
Use a potholder to remove from the toaster oven and place on a plate.
Top with the options listed above.

DIRECTIONS:

Slice the bread into ½ inch thick pieces and set aside, if it is not already pre-sliced.

Add the eggs, milk, syrup, vanilla, cinnamon, salt, and beat until combined.

Melt 1 teaspoon of butter over medium heat in a frying pan. Dip a slice of bread into the egg mixture, coating the front and back.

Let the excess egg drip off, then add to the frying pan. Repeat with another piece(s) if two pieces of bread can fit in the pan.

Fry on each side for 2-3 minutes, lower the heat if it begins to smoke or burn. Press the spatula onto the bread to make sure it has firmed up. It will be golden brown and not look like a wet sponge. Remove from the pan and place onto a plate.

Add another pat of butter then repeat steps 3-7 with the other slices of bread.

Top with the options listed above.

Apple Cinnamon Oatmeal

Oatmeal is a great anytime food. However, buying the sugar-filled packets is not the healthiest idea. Instead, buy plain quick oats in a canister — not only is it healthier, but it will save you money. You can always add your own sugar, spices, and toppings. I grew up on apple-cinnamon oatmeal packets and this is my homage to it. This tastes like the '80s but with less sugar!

Prep & cook time: 10 minutes, serves 1

INGREDIENTS:
½ c of plain **quick oats**
¼ of your favorite **apple**
1 tsp of **sugar** or drizzle of **maple syrup**
½ tsp of **cinnamon**
Pinch of kosher **salt**
1 c of **milk** of choice or **water**

NOTES

To boost the protein content, sprinkle hemp, chia, or flax seeds on top or add a spoonful of nut or sun butter.
A drizzle of olive oil adds some good healthy fat to the oatmeal

DIRECTIONS:
Add all the ingredients to the bowl and stir.
Microwave according to the directions on the package.
Stir and taste. Add more sweetener or liquid if needed.

DIRECTIONS:
Add the liquid and spices to a small pot. Place over medium heat and bring to a boil and stir occasionally.
Pour the oats and boil for 1 minute. Turn off the burner, remove the pot from the heat, and cover with a lid for 3 minutes.
Stir and taste. Add more sweetener or liquid if needed.

Smoothie Bowl

Prep time: 10 minutes, serves 1

INGREDIENTS:
¼ c plain Greek, plain, or non-dairy **yogurt**
½ c of **water**
¼ c of **frozen raspberries**
½ c of **frozen blueberries**
¼ c of **frozen strawberries**
¼ c of **frozen cherries**
¼ c of **frozen sliced peaches** or **½ banana**
1 **medjool date**, pit removed, or a shot of **maple syrup** or **honey**
One handful of **ice**

Optional Toppings:
* granola * shredded coconut * sliced almonds * chopped walnuts *
* chopped pecans * chia seeds * flax seeds * hemp seeds * strawberries *
* sliced bananas * raspberries * blackberries * blueberries * raisins *
* chopped dried apricots * dried cranberries * dried cherries *
* chopped dates *chocolate chips *

You can use as many of these fruits as you would like, you can even add fruit that is not listed. Buy a bag of mixed berries if you're short on freezer space. Or frozen packs of açaí and follow the instructions on the back. You can also replace the yogurt with 2 tablespoons of any nut or sun butter.

DIRECTIONS:
Add all of the ingredients into a blender and blend until it is a smooth and thick consistency.
Spoon the mixture into the bowl and smooth it out.
Top with any of the items listed above creating a cool design.
Post your bowl on social media because it is just so pretty and tag me? Maybe?

Berry Yogurt Parfait with Granola

Prep time: 10 minutes, makes 2 parfait cups

NOTES

A healthy alternative to flavored yogurts! The perfect breakfast or snack to make ahead and keep in your fridge.

INGREDIENTS:

¾ c of plain Greek, plain, or unsweetened non-dairy **yogurt**

Juice from ¼- ½ an orange or a splash of **orange juice**

A squeeze of **honey** or **maple syrup**

½ c of **berries**, if you use strawberries, chop them

½ c of **granola**

2 small **mason jars** with lids, small cups with a cover, or just put it in a bowl

Optional Toppings:

* chia seeds * flax seeds * chopped nuts * dark chocolate chips *

DIRECTIONS:

In a bowl, mix together yogurt, orange juice, and honey or maple syrup. Taste. Add more sweetener or juice if it is needed.

Cover the bottom of each mason jar or bowl with granola.

Add a spoonful of yogurt to cover the granola and top with some berries.

Sprinkle granola on top and repeat steps 2-4 until the jars, cups, or bowls are full.

Will keep in the fridge for 24-48 hours.

Chapter 2
SNACKS

Dorm Room Chocolatier: page 32

Guacamole

Prep time: 5 minutes, serves 1-2

INGREDIENTS:
1 ripe **avocado**
1 **lime**
Salt to taste
Tortilla chips or **veggies** for dipping

Add-in Options:
* 2 tsp of chopped cilantro
* 2 tsp of chopped tomato, seeded
* 1 tsp of finely chopped red onion
* 1 jalapeno, seeded and finely diced

NOTES

As a gentle reminder, please cut your avocado on a plate and not in your hand. And squeeze the pit out. Do not stab it with a knife. It may not end well for you. The pit will be fine.

DIRECTIONS:

Wash and dry the avocado, then cut it open and remove the pit by squeezing that half of the avocado into a bowl. The pit should pop out.

Mash the flesh of the avocado with a fork until smooth.

Slice lime it in half, then in half again, and you have quarters. See, there's that geometry making an appearance again. Squeeze a wedge into the bowl.

Sprinkle some salt and mix it all together. Taste to see if more salt or lime is needed.

Fold in any of the additional ingredients listed above.

Serve with tortilla chips and/or vegetables. Or with tacos and quesadillas (page 46), breakfast tacos or breakfast quesadillas (page 16), or pile it up on toast or crackers.

Popcorn in a Paper Bag

If you haven't heard, the microwave popcorn they sell in the stores is not wonderful due to the harmful chemicals in the bag as well as the ingredients that flavor the kernels. But what if you want to eat microwave popcorn in your dorm room like everyone else? Do not fret! Here is a safer recipe for you! You're welcome.

Prep & cook time: 5 minutes, serves 1

INGREDIENTS:
¼ c of **popcorn** kernels
A brown paper lunch bag
Salt and **melted butter**

> NOTES
> If you have a large 4 quart pot with a lid, see the instructions on the back of the bag or jar of popcorn kernels on how to cook it on your stovetop.

DIRECTIONS:

Add the popcorn to the bag and close it by folding the top over three times.

Microwave on high for 1-3 minutes or until the popping has realllly slowed down.

Remove from the microwave and carefully open the bag, it's hot and steamy and may even open some clogged pores.

Add some butter and salt in the bag.

Close the bag and shake it up so the butter and salt flavors the popcorn.

Eat out of the bag or pour into a bowl.

Apple Nachos

Prep time: 10 minutes, serves 1

INGREDIENTS:
1 **apple**, thinly sliced
1 handful of **granola**
2 tbsp of **nut** or **sun butter** -- if it's natural, you might need to
   microwave it in a ramekin to loosen it up

Optional Toppings:
* drizzle of maple syrup * drizzle of honey * chocolate chips * chopped nuts *
* hemp seeds * chia seeds * flax seeds * berries *

DIRECTIONS:
Arrange the sliced apples onn a plate - fanned out works best.
Drizzle the nut or sun butter over the apples.
Drizzle the syrup or honey over the apples.
Sprinkle granola and other toppings over the apples.

Mango Sorbet

Prep time: 10 minutes, serves 1

INGREDIENTS:
1 c of **frozen mango** chunks
Juice of 1 **orange** or a **splash of OJ**
Squeeze of **honey**

or make Frozen Mango Pops

Optional Toppings:
* raspberries * lime wedges * sliced strawberries * blueberries *
* shredded coconut *

DIRECTIONS:
Add the frozen mango, orange juice, and honey to the blender.
Blend on high, stopping periodically to free chunks of mango with a
spoon if they get stuck in the blades. Adding a little water can help
loosen them up.
Blend until the mixture is thick and smooth.
Spoon into cups.
Add toppings or eat it as is.

TIP: Freeze any leftovers in popsicle molds or yogurt squeezer containers.
Or lay out the mixture on a wax or parchment paper lined plate and freeze
for a couple of hours. Once frozen it becomes mango sorbet bark. Have
paper Dixie cups and toothpicks? Pour the extra mixture into the cups,
insert a toothpick, and pop in the freezer for 6 hours. Peel the paper off
the sorbet and you have a mini mango popsicle. This may seem strange, but
this is what I did as a kid and it was cool, man. It was cool!

Dorm Room Chocolatier

Before I opened What's in the Fridge? I worked at a chocolatier in Beverly Hills and Malibu. I sold all kinds of chocolates and one of the most popular treats was chocolate covered strawberries. Melting chocolate is easy, quick, and will impress your friends. Here are some healthy alternatives to candy to keep in your fridge or freezer: chocolate covered strawberries, frozen chocolate banana bites, and stuffed dates.

Prep time: 10 minutes, serves 1-4 people

INGREDIENTS:

A small package of **strawberries**, washed and dried

1 **banana**

6-12 **medjool dates** -- depends how many prepared stuffed dates you want to eat or keep in your fridge

Nut or sun butter

1 c of **chocolate chips** - if you are making all of the above at once, otherwise, a handful will do

Sea salt

DIRECTIONS for CHOCOLATE COVERED STRAWBERRIES:

Place the chocolate chips in a microwave-safe bowl and heat in 10-second increments, stirring in between, until melted. This should take a minute or less.

Hold the strawberry at the top, dip into the chocolate, and let the excess drip off. Place on a wax or parchment paper lined plate.

Refrigerate for 20 minutes or until the chocolate has hardened.

Eat now or store in an airtight container. These are good for 1-2 days.

DIRECTIONS for FROZEN CHOCOLATE BANANA BITES:

Slice the banana and place in a single layer on a wax or parchment paper lined plate or tray that will fit in your freezer.

Place the chocolate chips into a microwave-safe bowl and heat in 10-second increments, stirring in between until melted. It should take a minute or less.

Use a spoon to drizzle the chocolate over the bananas.

Put the plate in the freezer for 1-2 hours or until the chocolate and the bananas have hardened.

To store, place the banana bites in a freezer-safe resealable bag and keep in the freezer.

NOTES

Sweet, savory, energy stuffed dates! In a dorm fridge near you!

Skip the candy! These high-fiber, protein bites will be the best Study Buddy!

DIRECTIONS for STUFFED DATES:

Remove the pits from the dates by slicing open the dates and... removing the pit.

Fill each date with nut or sun butter and place on a wax or parchment paper lined plate.

Place the chocolate chips into a microwave-safe bowl and heat in 10-second increments, stirring in between until melted. It should take a minute or less.

Drizzle the chocolate over the dates then sprinkle with sea salt.

Refrigerate for 20 minutes or until the chocolate has hardened.

Store the extras in a resealable bag or an airtight container in the fridge for up to three days.

Still have extra chocolate? Dip pretzel twists or rods into the chocolate and lay them on the wax or parchment paper. Or lay the pretzels on the wax or parchment paper and drizzle chocolate over them. You can add sprinkles, melted peanut butter, or crushed cookies on top. Chill in the fridge for 20 minutes or until hardened. Store in resealable bag or airtight container for up to a week.

Or toss some mixed nuts into the chocolate and stir to coat. Lay them on the wax or parchment paper and place in the fridge to harden. Store in a resealable bag or airtight container. Will keep for a week in the fridge.

Yogurt Bark with Strawberries & Chocolate

Prep time: 30 minutes, serves 1

INGREDIENTS:
½ c of plain Greek, or plain, or non-dairy **yogurt**
A drizzle of **honey** or **maple syrup**
A handful of chopped **strawberries**
A handful of **chocolate chips**

A Healthy
Sub for
Ice Cream

DIRECTIONS:

Line a plate or tray with wax or parchment paper.
Place the chocolate chips into a microwave-safe bowl and heat in 10-second increments, stirring in between, until melted. This should take about a minute or less.
In another small bowl, sweeten the yogurt with honey or syrup, and taste. Then adjust if need be.
Add in the strawberries and mash with a fork so the flavors marry.
Spread the yogurt in a thin layer onto the lined plate or tray.
Drizzle the chocolate over the yogurt.
Place the plate or tray into the freezer for an hour or until the bark has hardened.
Remove and break into pieces.
Eat now or store the pieces in a resealable bag and keep in the freezer for a sweet, protein-packed treat!

Do not put the yogurt spoon into melted chocolate, it will cause the chocolate to seize up – which means it will harden up and is no longer a liquid.

Toaster Oven Cookie Pie

Prep & cook time: 30 minutes, serves 1-6

INGREDIENTS:
1 package of store-bought **cookie mix**
1 **egg**
1 stick of **butter**, softened

Also, if you don't want to buy cookie mix, you can buy refridgerated cookie dough

DIRECTIONS:
Preheat your toaster oven to 350 degrees.
In a medium-sized bowl mix softened butter, an egg, and the cookie mix until well combined. If the butter gets difficult to mix through, use your hands.
Crumple up a piece of parchment paper to line your 8-inch cake pan. Crumpling the paper makes it easier to place in the pan.
Add the cookie dough to the pan and using a spoon or your hands, evenly spread the dough in the pan.
Bake for 20 minutes. Use a toothpick to test to see if the cookie pie is cooked. The toothpick should come out clean.
Remove from the toaster oven with a potholder and place on a folded dishtowel or trivet as to not to burn any surfaces.
Let it cool for 10 minutes before cutting into it.

Charcuterie Board

NOTES

Here is a fun way to clean out your fridge and pantry and avoid waste! Pairs well with good friends!

Prep time: 10-15 minutes, serves 1-4

INGREDIENTS:

Cheese: 2-3 different ones; brie, gouda, goat, manchego, and cheddar
Deli meat: salami, prosciutto and other cured meat
Crackers
Condiment: jam, jelly, honey, dip, or mustard
Hummus or ranch dressing
Fruits: a combination of fresh and dried
Nuts or **dried chickpeas**
Olives or **pickles**
Chocolate anything
Large plate or cheeseboard

All of these items are suggestions, feel free to use anything that you would like.

Get creative, this is art!

DIRECTIONS:

Place the ramekins that are filled with condiments and savories in the center of the board.
To make a salami rose: use a small ramekin and overlap the salami pieces along the edges until there is no more room. Roll up a piece of salami and place it in the center of the rose. Place in the center of the plate or board as well.
For the prosciutto: drape it on the board like a wave or wrap it around a long breadstick or a piece of melon.
For a round of brie: slice like a pie or you can fan out the triangle pieces. If you have a triangle piece of brie, leave as is and place on the plate or board.
For a log of goat cheese: roll it in everything seasoning, chopped nuts, dried fruit, or drizzle with honey.

For the manchego: lay it on its side and cut off the black wax. Then cut it into ¼ inch triangles. Fan them out or alternate them so they stand up.

For the gouda and cheddar: leave as is or take your knife and chisel out chunks of cheese to sit next to the big block of cheese on the plate or board.

Use the remainder of the ingredients to fill in the blank spaces of the plate or board.

Serve and enjoy!

Mediterranean Plate

This is the easiest thing to throw together that packs protein, carbs, fruit, and veg all on one plate. Perfect as a meal or a snack.

Prep time: 5 minutes, serves 1

INGREDIENTS:
1 container of **hummus**
1 container of **tzatziki**
Cubes of **feta** or crumbled feta
Pita chips or **pita bread** cut into triangles
Olives
Cherry tomatoes
Cucumber slices

Optional Toppings:
* marinated red peppers * artichoke hearts * carrots * celery * dates *

DIRECTIONS:

Place the dips, marinated vegetables, and cheese into ramekins and then onto the plate. Or leave them in their container.

Add the vegetables and pita onto the plate.

Create flavor bombs by mixing and matching the flavors onto a triangle of pita or on a pita chip.

Chapter 3
LUNCH & DINNER

Romaine Caesar Boat: page 40

My Answer to Ramen

Prep & cook time: 5-10 minutes, serves 1

INGREDIENTS:

1 c of boxed or canned **broth** -- chicken, beef, or vegetable

A small handful of **angel hair pasta**, broken in half

Salt and **pepper** to taste

DIRECTIONS:

Pour the broth into a 12-14 oz mug, about halfway full, along with the broken pieces of angel hair pasta. Cook in the microwave for 2-4 minutes or until the broth is hot and the pasta is cooked.

Or in a small pot over medium heat, add 8 oz of broth along with the broken pieces of angel hair pasta and cook for 2-4 minutes or until the broth is hot and the pasta is cooked.

Season to taste and blow on it. It's hot!

Note: Add a handful of frozen vegetables and beans to make a quick vegetable noodle soup. Or add chicken and frozen vegetables for a super quick chicken noodle soup!

I know it's sacrilege to forgo ramen in college but this is my healthy alternative!

NOTES

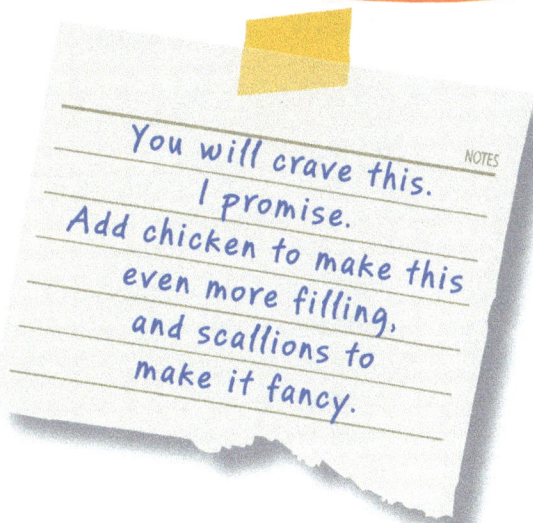

Noodles & Peanut Sauce

Prep & cook time: 15 minutes, serves 1

INGREDIENTS:

1 c of cooked **spaghetti**
¼ c of smooth **peanut butter**
¼ c of **water**
2 tbsp of **soy sauce** or **tamari**
½ tsp of **garlic powder**
1-1 ½ tsp of **ground ginger**
½-1 **lime**, juiced - extra lime for garnish
2 tsp of **honey**
¼ c of **peanuts**, crushed
Splash of **sesame oil** - optional
A pinch of **chili flakes** - optional

You will crave this. I promise. Add chicken to make this even more filling, and scallions to make it fancy.

NOTES

DIRECTIONS:

Cook the spaghetti in either the microwave or the stovetop, see page 60.
While the pasta cooks, add the peanut butter to a liquid measuring cup or a microwave-safe bowl. Heat the peanut butter for 15-30 seconds until it is loose.
Add the remaining ingredients to the peanut butter and stir. Taste and adjust seasoning if needed. This should yield ½ cup of sauce.
Once the pasta is cooked, drain, but leave a little water at the bottom.
Add half of the sauce to the noodles and combine. Taste. Add more, or leave it as it.
Pour the noodles into a bowl and top with crushed peanuts. Or chicken, scallions, and red chili flakes. Garnish with a lime wedge.

Chicken Teriyaki Bowl with Broccoli

Prep & cook time: 10-15 minutes, serves 1

INGREDIENTS:

1 c of cooked **chicken** or **protein of your choice** -- rotisserie chicken, leftover grilled chicken, steak, shrimp, or tofu
½ c cooked **rice** or uncooked jasmine rice
A handful of **broccoli florets** -- fresh or frozen -- or a different vegetable(s)
Teriyaki sauce
Sesame seeds -- optional

Get fancy and sauté the broccoli instead of steaming. Directions below. Or cook your own chicken breast and chop it up and add to the bowl

DIRECTIONS:

Cook the rice according to the directions on the package.
Follow the cooking instructions on the package for the frozen broccoli florets. For the fresh florets, place them in a microwave-safe bowl with an inch of water for 2-4 minutes until tender.
Heat the chicken for 30 seconds, then drizzle with teriyaki sauce.
Mix together then heat 10-20 seconds in the microwave or until hot.
To plate, place the rice in the bowl and add the chicken and broccoli on top.
Sprinkle with sesame seeds. You have a social-media-worthy dinner!

DIRECTIONS:

Cook the rice according to the package directions.
Follow the cooking instructions on the package for the frozen broccoli florets. For the fresh florets, place them in a small pot with an inch of water and cook over low-medium heat for 2-4 minutes or until tender. Drain the water.
Add the chicken to the pot with the broccoli and toss with a drizzle teriyaki sauce until hot.
See steps 5-6 under microwave.

NOTES

This dish works great with leftover rice and veggies from your last take-out delivery order

Sauté the broccoli in a tablespoon of olive or sesame oil in a frying pan over medium heat for 5-10 minutes or until it is soft. If the pan starts to get a little brown, add a splash of water and scrape the brown bits up — that is fond and it is flavor! The water will also help steam the broccoli. Then add the chicken and a drizzle or more of teriyaki sauce to the pan and heat through. Add the cooked rice to a bowl and place the chicken and broccoli on top. Sprinkle sesame seeds and sliced scallions on top.

Feeling adventurous, turn this into fried rice by adding a scrambled egg (see page 13), scallions, soy or tamari sauce instead of teriyaki sauce, and add some ground ginger. Finely chop the proteins and vegetables and toss with the rice, eggs, scallions, and soy sauce.

Chopped Vegetable Salad

Prep time: 10 minutes, serves 1

INGREDIENTS:

1 **cucumber**, diced
1 medium **tomato**, seeded and diced
 or a handful of cherry tomatoes, quartered
½ **bell pepper,** diced
A handful of **olives**, halved or chopped
¼ c of **garbanzo beans**
½ **avocado**, diced
A handful of **romaine leaves**, chopped
A handful of **crumbled feta**
1-2 tbsp of **extra virgin olive oil**
A splash of **red wine vinegar**
¼ tsp of **sea salt** and a few cranks of **black pepper**

Optional Toppings:
* marinated artichoke hearts * roasted red peppers * dried oregano *

Make this salad ahead of time in mason jars - dressing on the bottom and salad on top. Cover and store in the fridge. When you are ready to eat, shake it up and enjoy!

DIRECTIONS:

Place all of the ingredients into the mixing bowl and toss to combine.
Taste for seasoning.
Eat now or store in the fridge until ready to serve. FYI, the salt will draw out the liquid from your vegetables after it sits for a while.

Mixed Greens with Homemade Vinaigrette

Prep time: 10 minutes, serves 1

INGREDIENTS for SALAD:
1 bag or container of **mixed greens** -- just need a couple of handfuls
A few **cherry tomatoes** and **cucumber slices**
1 carrot, shaved -- use your vegetable peeler or they can be sliced

Add-Ins & Optional Toppings:
* other vegetables you like * cheese * beans * meat * apple slices * berries *
* nuts * sunflower seeds * pepitas (pumpkin seeds) *

INGREDIENTS for DRESSING:
1 tbsp of **vinegar** -- balsamic, apple cider, or red wine
¼ c of **extra virgin olive oil**
1 tsp of **Dijon mustard** or **plain Greek yogurt** -- optional
A squeeze of **honey** or **maple syrup**
A splash of **water**
A pinch of kosher or sea **salt** and a few cranks of **pepper**

DIRECTIONS for DRESSING:
Add the vinegar, sweetener of choice, water, and mustard or yogurt to a mason jar and close with the lid. Shake well until combined.
Add olive oil, salt and pepper, close the lid and shake until combined.
Taste and add more seasoning if need be.

DIRECTIONS for SALAD:
Add the salad ingredients to a bowl.
Pour the desired amount of dressing on top and toss to coat.
Add any toppings from the list above and enjoy!

Tacos & Quesadillas

Prep & cook time: 5-10 minutes, serves 1

INGREDIENTS for TACOS:
2-3 flour, corn, or gluten-free **tortillas**
Protein of choice: rotisserie chicken, chopped up leftover hamburger, steak, shrimp, fish, tofu, or vegetables
shredded or sliced Monterey Jack or cheddar **cheese**

Add-Ins and Optional Toppings:
* avocado slices * guacamole * chopped tomato * sour cream * cilantro * salsa *

DIRECTIONS:

Gather all of the taco ingredients. If your proteins or vegetables need to be heated up, do so and set aside.
To heat up the tortillas, wrap them in a damp paper towel and microwave for 5-10 seconds. Or place them in the toaster oven to heat until just warm.
Remove the tortillas and add the filling, evenly distributing it to each taco.
Top the tacos with the options from the list above.

INGREDIENTS for QUESADILLAS:
2 flour, corn, or gluten-free **tortillas**
½ c of shredded or 2 slices of cheddar and/or Monterey Jack **cheese**
1-2 tsp of **butter** -- for the frying pan only

Add-Ins and Optional Toppings:
* chicken * baby spinach * sautéed onions & peppers * salsa *
* avocado slices * guacamole * sour cream * cilantro * scallions *

DIRECTIONS:

On a plate, add a tortilla topped with cheese, leaving a border around the edges, plus any add-ins.
Place into the microwave for 5-10 seconds or until the cheese is just about melted. Careful not to cook for too long or the tortilla will dry out.
Remove from the microwave and fold the tortilla in half and cut into triangles.
Serve with the toppings options listed above.

DIRECTIONS:

Place a tortilla on aluminum foil or parchment paper. Sprinkle ¼ cup of the cheese on the tortilla, leaving a border around the edges and add the chicken, spinach, onions, peppers, to the cheese.

Toast for a minute or until just melted.

Remove from the toaster and fold the tortilla in half. If you want it crispier, toast for another minute or until golden brown on top – don't burn it! Cut it in half or into 4 triangles.

Repeat with the rest of the tortillas. Serve with toppings.

DIRECTIONS:

Pre-heat frying pan on medium and add a teaspoon of butter to the pan, or cooking spray to coat the pan.

Add a tortilla – if you can fit two, add two – and evenly spread a ¼ cup of cheese on each tortilla, leaving a border around the edges. Plus, any of the add-in optional ingredients mentioned above.

Cook for 2 minutes until the cheese is melted.

Gently fold the tortilla and flatten it down and cook for a minute more.

Flip the quesadilla over and cook for another minute on the other side. The goal is to achieve crispiness on each side.

Remove from the pan and place on a plate and cut it in half or into triangles.

Repeat with the rest of the tortillas. Serve with toppings.

Dorm Room Nachos

Prep & cook time: 15 minutes, serves 1

INGREDIENTS:
½ c of shredded **chicken** --rotisserie chicken is
  perfect for this -- optional avocado, diced
½ c of shredded cheddar or Monterey Jack
  cheese
A couple of handfuls of **tortilla chips**

Optional Toppings:
* sliced black olives * sliced jalapenos * black beans * salsa *
* chopped tomato * sour cream * lime wedges *

DIRECTIONS:
On a microwave-safe plate or an aluminum foil or parchment paper lined
toaster oven tray, lay the tortilla chips in a single layer and sprinkle
some of the cheese and chicken on top.
Add another layer of chips on top and sprinkle the remaining cheese and
chicken on top.
Heat in the microwave for 30 seconds or in the toaster oven for a few
minutes until the cheese has melted.
Top your nachos with the options listed above.
Great for one person, but even better to share with friends!

NOTES
This is a forgiving dish,
you do not have to
measure or use all the
suggested ingredients.
Do what you like!

Stuffed Baked Potato

Prep & cook time: 10-45 minutes, serves 1

INGREDIENTS:
1 **Russet potato** -- the brown one with the roughish skin
Butter, cheese, sour cream
A handful of frozen or fresh **broccoli florets**
Salt & pepper to taste
Water

DIRECTIONS:

Wash and dry the potato, then use a sharp knife to poke holes in the potato so the steam can escape during the cooking process. This will keep it from exploding!

Place on a microwave-safe plate and cook for 6-8 minutes.

How to know it's cooked – first, no joke, HOT POTATO! Handle it like... a hot potato. Use a potholder to hold the potato and carefully cut a slit across the top. If it cuts open easily and the potato is easy to mash, it is cooked. Enjoy the steamy facial. Food is magic.

To cook in a toaster oven, bake at 400 degrees for 45-60 minutes on an oven-safe tray or on aluminum foil. This will yield a crispy exterior. The potato is done when the outside is crispy it gives a little when it is squeezed.

Mash the potato in the skin then add butter, cheese, and salt.

Next, prepare the frozen broccoli according to package or the fresh florets in a microwave-safe bowl with an inch of water for 2-4 minutes or until the broccoli is tender. Then add on top of the potato.

Grilled Cheese & Tomato Soup

There is nothing better than settling in with a crunchy, gooey grilled cheese and a cozy bowl or mug of tomato soup. In my senior year of college, my friend taught me how to make a grilled cheese this way and I truly believe it is the only way to do it. It would not be very nice of me if I were to gate-keep this from you while you are in school. So here you go.

Prep time & cook time: 10-15 minutes, serves 1

INGREDIENTS for TOMATO SOUP:
¼ c of **marinara sauce**
½-¾ c of **vegetable** or **chicken stock**
Salt and **pepper** to taste

DIRECTIONS:

Blend the broth and the sauce until they are smooth. Pour the blended soup into a microwave-safe mug or bowl and heat for 30 seconds to a minute or until it is hot.
Or pour the blended soup into a small pot and simmer on medium to low heat for 3-5 minutes or until hot.
Season with salt and pepper to taste.
This will keep for three days in the fridge and six months in the freezer.
If you have basil, pesto, or parmesan cheese, add that to the soup. A splash of half and half will add creaminess and richness.

INGREDIENTS for GRILLED CHEESE:
2 pieces of **sandwich bread**
¼ c of **shredded cheddar cheese**
¼ c of **shredded Monterey Jack cheese**
1 tbsp of **butter**

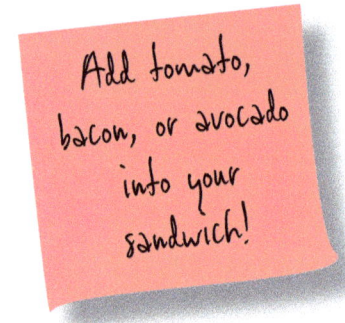

Add tomato, bacon, or avocado into your sandwich!

DIRECTIONS:

Pre-heat toaster oven to 350 degrees.
Butter each piece of bread and place the buttered side down on an aluminum foil or parchment paper lined toaster oven tray.
Sprinkle the cheese evenly on one piece and add the other piece on top, buttered side up.
Bake for 2-3 minutes until cheese is melted and bubbly, and the bread is toasty.

Remove and use a spatula to flip it over and bake for another 2 minutes or until toasty.

Remove from the toaster once golden and melty, and place on a plate and cut diagonally, obviously.

Serve with tomato soup. Or chips and a pickle.

DIRECTIONS:

Pre-heat the frying pan on medium-low and add 2 teaspoons of butter to coat the pan.

Butter each side of the bread and place one piece, buttered side down into the pan.

Sprinkle the cheese evenly on that piece and add the other piece of bread on top, buttered side up.

Cook for 2-3 minutes or until the cheese starts to melt.

Flip the grilled cheese over and cook for another 2-3 minutes.

Add a little more butter to crisp up the edges. Cook until the cheese is melty and the bread is crunchy. The goal here is to keep the sandwich from smoking, which is why it is on a low-ish heat.

See steps 6-7 under **toaster oven**.

Wraps, Pockets, Roll-Ups, & Romaine Boats

Prep time: 10 minutes, serves 1

INGREDIENTS:
Choose a vessel:
2 tortillas, 1 **flatbread wrap**, 1 **pita pocket**, or
   4 large **romaine leaves**

Choose your toppings:
* deli meat * chicken * steak * hummus * cheese * cucumber slices *
* cherry tomatoes - cut in half * shredded carrots * bell peppers strips *
* olives * marinated artichoke hearts * canned beans * sliced avocado *
* olive oil * red wine vinegar * balsamic vinegar * ranch dressing *
* Italian dressing * Caesar dressing * mustard * mayo * sea salt *
* everything bagel seasoning * black pepper * oregano * sesame seeds *
* red chili flakes *

DIRECTIONS:
First, figure out what flavor combo to make. See ideas below.
Mise en place the tools and ingredients. That's French for "get the
materials out of the fridge and storage bins and create an assembly line."
Lay out the vessels – tortillas, lettuce leaves, etc. - on your plate.
Fill the vessel with anything from the toppings list.

Flavor Combo Ideas:
Romaine Caesar boat with croutons, black pepper, parmesan cheese, Caesar dressing
Tortilla ranch wrap with chicken, cheddar, tomato, lettuce, avocado, ranch dressing
Pita pocket with turkey, romaine, Swiss, tomato
Tortilla wrap with beans, cheese, tomato, avocado
Flat bread wrap with cold cuts, lettuce, tomato, onion, olive oil, vinegar, salt, pepper, oregano
Romaine boat with cucumber, bell pepper, olives, feta, oregano, olive oil, red wine vinegar, salt, pepper or just use Italian dressing.
Romaine boat with carrots, bell pepper, avocado, cucumber, sesame ginger dressing, sesame seeds

Romaine Caesar Boat (top) & Tortilla Ranch Wrap

Pizzafy!

Prep & cook time: 10 minutes, serves 1

Here are 4 of my favorite ways to enjoy some pizza

INGREDIENTS:
1 **bagel**, sliced in half or 1-2 **tortillas**
  - flour or gluten-free, corn will not work
2 spoonfuls of **marinara sauce**
2 handfuls of shredded **mozzarella** or a slice of mozzarella
  - for each bagel half or tortilla
Dried **oregano** and/ or **red chili flakes**

DIRECTIONS for PIZZA BAGEL:

Place the bagel halves facing up on a plate, or on aluminum foil, or a parchment paper lined toaster oven tray.
Spread a thin layer of sauce on each half, then sprinkle cheese on top.
Microwave for 15-30 seconds or until the cheese is melted.
Or place in the toaster oven and cook at 350 degrees for 5 minutes or until the cheese is melted.
Sprinkle with oregano and/or red chili flakes.
Enjoy and also wonder why this is not sold everywhere!

DIRECTIONS for PIZZA ROLLS, PIZZADILLA and VERY THIN PIZZA

Place the tortilla on a plate, or on aluminum foil, or a parchment paper lined toaster oven tray.
Spread a thin layer of sauce, leaving a border around the edges.
Sprinkle the cheese on the tortilla, leaving a border around the edges.
Place in the microwave for 10-20 seconds, or in the toaster oven at 350 degrees for 2-5 minutes or until the cheese is just melted.
Sprinkle with oregano and/or red chili flakes.
For the pizza roll, start at one end and roll up the tortilla like you would a piece of paper to turn into a microphone.
Cut the roll in half. The cheese should be ooey, and gooey.
Repeat with the other tortilla(s).
For the pizzadilla, fold the cooked tortilla in half and cut into triangles.
For the very thin pizza, cut it like a pizza.

Avery's Mediterranean Pita Pizza

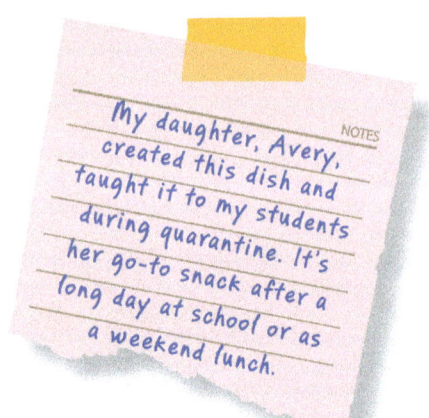

My daughter, Avery, created this dish and taught it to my students during quarantine. It's her go-to snack after a long day at school or as a weekend lunch.

NOTES

Prep time: 10 minutes, serves 1

INGREDIENTS:
1 **pita**
1 small **tomato**, chopped or cherry tomatoes, quartered
¼ of a **bell pepper**, washed, dried, and diced
¼ of a **cucumber**, washed, dried, seeded, and diced
1-2 tbsp of **hummus**
A sprinkle of crumbled **feta cheese**
Salt, pepper, and **oregano** to taste

Optional Toppings:
* drizzle of olive oil * a splash of red wine vinegar *
* kalamata or black olives * thinly sliced red onion *
* roasted red peppers * marinated artichoke hearts *

DIRECTIONS:

Place all of the chopped vegetables into a bowl or a mason jar with a lid.

Add the salt, pepper, oregano, feta, and mix with a spoon or shake it up in the jar.

Warm the pita in the microwave for 5 seconds or toast in the toaster oven until warm.

Place the pita on a plate and spread on the hummus.

Top with the vegetable mix, but not too much as the pita will break!

Cut the pizza into triangles or fold in half to eat.

Don't have any vegetables left but just have feta and hummus? That's okay, because pita, hummus, and feta taste great together!

Pasta!
Simple
Marinara

Prep & cook time: 10 minutes, serves 1-2

INGREDIENTS:
1 handful of **spaghetti**
½ c of **pasta sauce**
Parmesan cheese

DIRECTIONS:

You can make the pasta in the microwave, see pg 60. Once al dente, add sauce and heat some more

Boil -- But first, how to boil water for pasta:
Add water 3/4 the way to the top of the pot
and turn the heat on high. Once the water is boiling - a lot of bubbles
popping up - add 1 tablespoon of salt to the water to flavor your pasta.
Follow the instructions on the box of pasta, and in my opinion, always cook
it al dente. Al dente means "to the tooth" - meaning, the pasta remains firm.
Basically, do not overcook your pasta and turn it into mush.
Cook the pasta and reserve 1/2 cup of the pasta water before draining it.
Add the pasta back to the pot as well as the desired amount of sauce.
Over low heat, toss the pasta and sauce together and cook until the pasta is
less firm, but not mush. Use a little of the pasta water if the sauce needs
to be looser.
Sprinkle parmesan and mix through.
Serve and top with more parmesan. There is no such thing as too much cheese.
If someone tells you this, they are not your friend!

Easy pasta meal ideas:
* butter & salt * veggie pasta * meat sauce * cottage cheese & salt *
* chicken nugget parm & pasta * meatballs * olive oil & Parmesan *
* deconstructed lasagna: ricotta, parmesan, mozzarella, & marinara *

Penne Caprese

Prep & cook time: 10 minutes, serves 1

Here's a twist on the classic caprese salad. Instead of fresh basil, a jar of pesto will do the trick. You can even add other roasted vegetables to the dish to make it an even heartier meal. Wanna get really creative? Buy fancy toothpicks and skewer a cherry tomato, mozzarella ball, and any shaped pasta and lay them on a platter and serve with a pesto dipping sauce.

NOTES
Make ahead of time and store in mason jars for a quick grab-and-go lunch or dinner!

PS:
See page 60 to make pasta in the microwave

INGREDIENTS:
1 c of **penne pasta**
¼ - ½ c of prepared **pesto**
A couple of **fresh mozzarella balls**, torn or chopped
1 small **tomato**, diced, or a handful of
    cherry tomatoes, halved

DIRECTIONS:

Cook the pasta according to package. Reserve some pasta water on the side.
Add the pesto to a bowl along with the pasta and toss. To make it saucier, add some of the pasta water.
Sprinkle the tomato and mozzarella on top.
Enjoy!

Easy Mac 'N Cheese

A healthier version than the box brands! It tastes better and uses all real ingredients.

Prep & cook time: 5-10 minutes, serves 1

INGREDIENTS:
½ c of **dry macaroni**
¾ c of **sharp cheddar cheese**, shredded
½ tbsp of **butter**
4 tbsp of **milk**
½ tsp of **salt**
Water

To elevate it, add chicken or steamed broccoli. Try some hot sauce or cayenne pepper. Or crumble some croutons for crunch on top.

DIRECTIONS:

Place the macaroni in a bowl and cover with water and a ½ teaspoon of salt. Cook on high for 3 minutes or until the pasta is al dente (firm, but not mush).
Drain the pasta if there's any water left. It is okay if some water remains.
Add the butter, ½ of the cheese, and 2 tablespoons of the milk then stir.
Place back in the microwave and heat for a minute.
Remove and add the rest of the milk and cheese and stir. Taste and season if need be.

DIRECTIONS:

Put the macaroni in a pot with salt, cover with water and bring to a boil. Stir every couple of minutes. This should take 7 minutes.
Once cooked, if there is any remaining water, drain the pasta water into the sink.
Add butter, 2 tablespoon of milk and ½ of the cheese to the mac and stir.
Add the remaining cheese and milk and stir. Taste and season if need be.

Chapter 4
DRINKS

Berry Smoothie: page 67

A Basic Latte

Okay, let's be honest, no one is making espresso in their rooms. So do not come after with me the semantics on the names of the coffee drinks below and the foam to steamed milk ratio. I am just trying to help you save $5+ a day and still enjoy a hot or cold, frothy, caffeinated bevvy.

Prep time: 5 minutes, serves 1

Served hot or iced with foam!

INGREDIENTS for A BASIC LATTE:
Makes 1 **8 oz cup**
1-2 **shots of espresso** or ½ c of coffee
¼ c of any kind of **milk**
ice -- if you are making an iced drink

DIRECTIONS for FROTHER MACHINE:
Pour the coffee into the mug or tumbler.
Add ¼ cup of milk to the machine and hit the appropriate drink setting.
If making an iced drink, make the coffee stronger than usual because the ice will dilute the drink.
If using any type of sweetener, add that to the bottom of the cup or glass, then the hot coffee and stir. This is a whole "chemistry-molecules, cold vs. hot thing" – this was taught in class – if you remember and were not texting with some friends a few seats over.
If making an iced drink, add ice to the tumbler, then coffee, then top with cold foam.
If making a hot latte, add the foam to the top of your drink.
Sit back and sip your fancy drink knowing it cost a buck and five minutes. It will make the coffee that much richer and you, too!

DIRECTIONS for ELECTRIC HANDHELD WHISK/FROTHER:
Pour the coffee into the mug or tumbler.
Add ¼ cup of milk to the coffee and using the electric hand whisk, lower it to just below the surface and press "low." It will foam in about 3 seconds.
Note, The higher fat content of the milk, the thicker the foam will be.

Make sure not to fill the milk to the top because there needs to be room for air to build in the milk. It will make a huge mess otherwise. I tested this theory. Take my word. Take the word of my kitchen counter, if it could talk.

Mocha & Caramel Latte

Add a teaspoon of chocolate syrup or caramel syrup to the bottom of the coffee cup. If using cacao powder, different than hot chocolate mix, add a teaspoon of maple syrup, trust me on this combo. Then add the hot coffee and stir.
For an iced drink, if using syrup, make stripes in your glass like they do at the coffee shops and top with whipped cream, either from a canister or fresh whipped cream found on page 64.

Pumpkin Spice Latte

How can this be a faux coffee shop without a pumpkin spice latte? A container of pumpkin pie spice can be found in the spice section of the grocery store - add ½ teaspoon to your coffee along with 1-2 teaspoons of maple syrup or sugar, a dash of vanilla extract, and stir. Add milk or half and half, then use your electric handheld whisk to blitz the drink for a few seconds until it foams. Sprinkle the foam with pumpkin pie spice. Or heat the milk up in a frother and then add to the hot coffee. This recipe is a healthier and less expensive version of a classic!

Maple Latte

Maple syrup in coffee sounds weird but honestly, it is great! Try it. Just add 1-2 teaspoons to hot coffee or to the milk in the frother, voila!

Chai Tea Latte

Let's talk about chai tea lattes. They are so comforting but can be packed with added sugars and emulsifiers. Instead, buy chai tea bags to make the tea. Stir in a teaspoon of honey and a dash of vanilla extract. Pour in the milk and blend with an electric handheld whisk. **If drinking it iced**, make the tea stronger because the ice will dilute it. Earl Grey also makes for a great tea latte.

Hot Chocolate & Whipped Cream

Prep & cook time: 5-10 minutes, serves 1

INGREDIENTS for HOT CHOCOLATE:
1 tbsp of sweet **ground cocoa**, or **chocolate syrup**.
 If using 100% **raw cacao powder**, use 1 tbsp of powder with
 2 tsp of **maple syrup** or **sugar**
1 c of any kind of **milk**

INGREDIENTS for WHIPPED CREAM:
¼ c of **heavy cream** or 1 can of **coconut milk**
½ tsp of **powdered sugar, sugar,** or **maple syrup**

DIRECTIONS for HOT CHOCOLATE:

In a mug add the cocoa powder.
 Or the cacao powder and maple syrup. Or the chocolate syrup.
Add the milk and heat in the microwave for 30 seconds to 1 minute until
it is hot. Stir to make sure all the ingredients are incorporated.
For the stovetop, in a small pot over medium-low heat, add the cocoa
powder, or cacao powder and maple syrup, or chocolate syrup and stir
until combined. When bubbles form on the edges of the pot, it is ready.
Pour into a mug and enjoy!

DIRECTIONS for WHIPPED CREAM with HEAVY CREAM:

Pour ¼ cup of heavy cream into a mug.
Use the electric handheld whisk and whip the cream until it's fluffy -
should take less than a minute.
Add ½ teaspoon of powdered or table sugar and continue to whip until it
looks like shaving cream.

DIRECTIONS for WHIPPED CREAM with COCONUT MILK:

Open the can and scoop ½ of the cream that's on top
 into a mug. Save the liquid for a future smoothie.
See steps 2-3 from above.

Vegan Chocolate Shake

INGREDIENTS:
2 **medjool dates**, remove the pit
¼ of an **avocado**
½ of a **banana**
2 tsp of **raw cacao powder**, or **unsweetened cocoa powder**
A handful of **ice**
1 tbsp of **almond** or **peanut butter**
½ c of **water** or **almond milk**

DIRECTIONS:
In this order add water, banana, avocado, dates, almond or peanut butter, and cacao powder and blend until smooth.
Once blended, add ice, and blend until incorporated.
Taste and adjust sweetness if necessary.
Pour into a glass and enjoy!

If you do not have dates use a tablespoon of maple syrup or honey

Tropical Smoothie

Prep time: 5 minutes, serves 1

INGREDIENTS:
¼ c of **frozen pineapple** chunks
¼ c of **frozen mango**
½ c of **frozen peaches**
¼ of a **banana**
½ can of **coconut milk**
Splash of **orange juice** or **wate**r
A handful of **ice**

You can get creative and add strawberries, raspberries, frozen passion fruit cubes, or even guava nectar. This will mentally get you ready for your tropical spring break vacation and act as a great motivator to power through your midterms!

DIRECTIONS:
Blend together the ingredients until smooth. If the fruit gets stuck, add some water or orange juice to loosen up the fruit.
Pour into a glass and top with raw or toasted coconut if or an umbrella and a straw! I mean, it's college, of course you have accoutrements for drinks!

Berry Smoothie

INGREDIENTS:
¼ c of plain Greek, or plain, or plain non-dairy **yogurt**
½ c of **water**
1 c of **frozen berries** of any kind
1 **medjool date** - pit removed or a teaspoon of maple syrup or honey
Handful of **ice**

Optional Add-in:
* 2 tbsp of nut or seed butter * hemp, chia, or flax seeds * fresh spinach *

DIRECTIONS:
Blend all the ingredients until it is a pinkish-purple color and smooth.
If the blades are not churning, the fruit could be stuck. While the
blender is stopped, use a spoon and move the contents around to release
from the blades. Add a little water to help loosen it up and continue
blending until smooth.
Taste and adjust sweetness if needed.
Pour into a glass and get to class! Or get back to studying!

Kitchen Essentials
For Your Dorm Room

To help you get organized I have included lists to stock your pantry (or storage bin), fridge, and freezer with items that coincide with the recipes.

You do not need all of these items all at once! Mark the recipes you would make given the space and equipment you have in your room. Then, build your shopping list. You can keep your kitchen tools in a storage bin under your bed, or in a hanging shoe sleeve in your closet.

Regarding spices, vinegar, and big bulk items such as sugar and salt - since aesthetic is queen, you can buy and take some ingredients from your parents' pantry.
Or when your parent/caregiver runs out of a spice, save the container and fill it up for college. (You can blame me for your foraging, I will take the fall for you – just tell them this is a money saving hack. Parents eat that up. I know. I am that parent.)

Kitchen Tools:

UTENSILS & KITCHENWARE:
[   ]   Paring or **small sharp knife**
[   ]   **Vegetable peeler**
[   ]   **Small strainer** (for beans, berries, rice, and pasta)
[   ]   Small **wood cutting board** (8x11)
[   ]   **Metal spatula** and **wooden spoon**
[   ]   **Cutlery** (fork, knife, spoon)
[   ]   **Microwave-safe plates** and **bowls**
[   ]   Reusable **stainless steel water bottles** and **bottle brush**
[   ]   **Glasses, microwave-safe mugs, straws**
[   ]   **Ice cube trays**
[   ]   1 set of **measuring cups** (liquid measuring cup is just fine)
[   ]   **Measuring spoons**
[   ]   Handheld **can opener**
[   ]   **Paper towels, dish soap, sponge, dish towel**
[   ]   **Aluminum foil, parchment paper, wax paper, plastic wrap**
[   ]   **Potholder**

COOKWARE & APPLIANCES:
[   ]   **Small blender**
[   ]   Small **coffee maker**
[   ]   **Water pitcher with filter**
[   ]   Small **pot with lid** and **8-inch skillet**
[   ]   **Microwave-safe ramekins** (6-8 oz)
        and/or **microwave-safe glass containers** with a lid
[   ]   8-inch round **stainless cake pan** (can be used to heat up food as well)
[   ]   **Toaster oven tray** (8x10)
[   ]   **Stainless steel milk frother** or **electric handheld whisk**

STORAGE:
[   ]   **Glass containers** and/or **mason jars**
[   ]   **Bags** (resealable & brown lunch bags)

Pantry Staples:

OILS, SPICES, ETC.

[ ] Extra virgin **olive oil**
[ ] Red wine/balsamic/apple cider **vinegar**
[ ] **Soy sauce**/tamari/teriyaki sauce
[ ] Kosher **salt**/sea salt/table salt
[ ] **Pepper** *(the disposable peppermills are great)*
[ ] **Garlic powder**
[ ] **Dried oregano**
[ ] **Red pepper flakes**
[ ] **Ground cinnamon**
[ ] Cane or brown **sugar**
[ ] **Coffee** and **Tea**

CANNED & DRY GOODS:

[ ] **Salsa** *(or fresh for the Fridge)*
[ ] **Canned beans**
[ ] **Pasta**
[ ] **Pasta sauce**
[ ] **Broth: Chicken** and/or **vegetable** *(boxed with resealable cap or small can)*
[ ] **Microwave-ready rice** or **Jasmine** or **Basmati** if you have a stove
[ ] **Popcorn kernels**
[ ] **Bread** *(tortillas, pitas, whole wheat/sourdough sliced bread, bagels)*
[ ] **Nut/seed butters** *(there are 2 kinds, shelf stable and non-shelf-stable. Try to choose ones with 2 ingredients or less)*
[ ] **Pure fruit preserves** *(fruit should be the first ingredient, sugar the second ingredient)*
[ ] Unsweetened **applesauce**
[ ] Quick cooking **oats**
[ ] **Nuts** *(almonds, cashews, peanuts, pecans, pistachios...)*
[ ] **Seeds** *(pumpkin, sunflower, hemp, chia, flax...)*
[ ] **Crackers, chips and cookies**

BAKING:

[ ] **Chocolate chips**
[ ] 100% **cacao powder** or **chocolate powder** or **syrup**
[ ] **Maple syrup** *(100% pure)* and/or **honey**
[ ] **Dried fruit** *(dates, cranberries, cherries, raisins, apricots)*
[ ] **Vanilla extract**

Fridge & Freezer Staples:

DAIRY:

[ ] **Eggs** or eggs in a re-sealable carton
[ ] **Cheese** (slices or blocks last longer than shredded and/or cheese sticks, shredded)
[ ] **Milk** and/or half and half
[ ] **Yogurt** (plain Greek because it can be used SO many different ways. Don't worry, I'll teach you how to sweeten it up!)
[ ] **Butter** (sticks and unsalted. Spreadable is made with oil. Of course, if you're dairy-free, do what works for you)

PREPARED FOOD:

[ ] **Hummus** (preferably made with Extra Virgin Olive Oil; EVOO)

PRODUCE:

[ ] **Veggies** (carrots, celery, bell peppers, cucumbers, cherry tomatoes, snap peas...)
[ ] **Fruit** (apples, pears, bananas, oranges, berries...)
[ ] **Greens** (Lettuce, spinach, and arugula are always good for making a quick salad)
[ ] **Avocados**

FREEZER:

[ ] **Frozen fruit** (great for smoothies or to snack on)
[ ] **Frozen veggies** (peas, broccoli, corn, edamame...)

You can freeze extra butter sticks. Extra broth can be frozen in ice cube trays

About Jill...

Jill lives in Los Angeles with her family. Her passion for cooking began when she was 8 years old and continued through high school when she begged her dad to let her open a restaurant. During college, she honed her cooking skills and started to shed her picky eating ways. Once she moved to Los Angeles and started hanging around the craft service table while working in television/film production, a whole new culinary world opened up to her. Jill put Hollywood on hold and starred in her new role as a stay-at-home-mom. After providing so many homemade snacks to her friends during play dates, her friends convinced her to start a personal chef business. What's in the Fridge? was born.

In addition to cooking for others, she started teaching cooking classes at her kitchen table, at her son's preschool, and then over Zoom during Covid. Jill continues to teach online cooking classes to kids, teens, and adults.

dinner is served

Jill, age 10

Acknowledgements

I would like to thank everyone who helped test recipes for this cookbook. To Jon, for having the arduous task of tasting everything I made and then helping me choose the pictures for the book. To my mom for the support and for testing everything in the microwave because mine was broken. And to my dad, thanks for tasting everything mom tested. To my helpful college student testers: Teddy, Alyssa, and Jocelyn -- your feedback was so helpful in making sure that I was providing the best possible recipes that could be made easily in a confined space.

Thank you to Sara for making sure my grammar is (or was?) correct and providing me with constructive real-mom-teacher advice. And to my cheerleader, Hilary-- thank you for always being supportive of my writing. To Robyn, my designer, who made my vision a reality and after a few weeks could read my mind and shift the post-it notes without me saying a word. Thank you for the laughs, challenging me to step up my photography game, and helping me access my creativity during the hardest time in my life. To my friend Mark, who encouraged me to make my pics more colorful and tutored me on how to properly color correct. And to Heather, my ready and willing graphic designer, who created my promotional materials.

To my son, who claps for me at each meal -- I thank you for being my biggest and most loyal fan. And to my daughter, if it were not for you, I would not have changed the way I look at food and how I was preparing it. You made me want to research ingredients and learn how to be a more creative and healthy cook. You and your brother are the reason I am the cook that I am today. Now go cook something delicious and think of me!

Index

...cont.

Index

www.ingramcontent.com/pod-product-compliance
Lightning Source LLC
Chambersburg PA
CBHW041123120626
46547CB00019B/2833